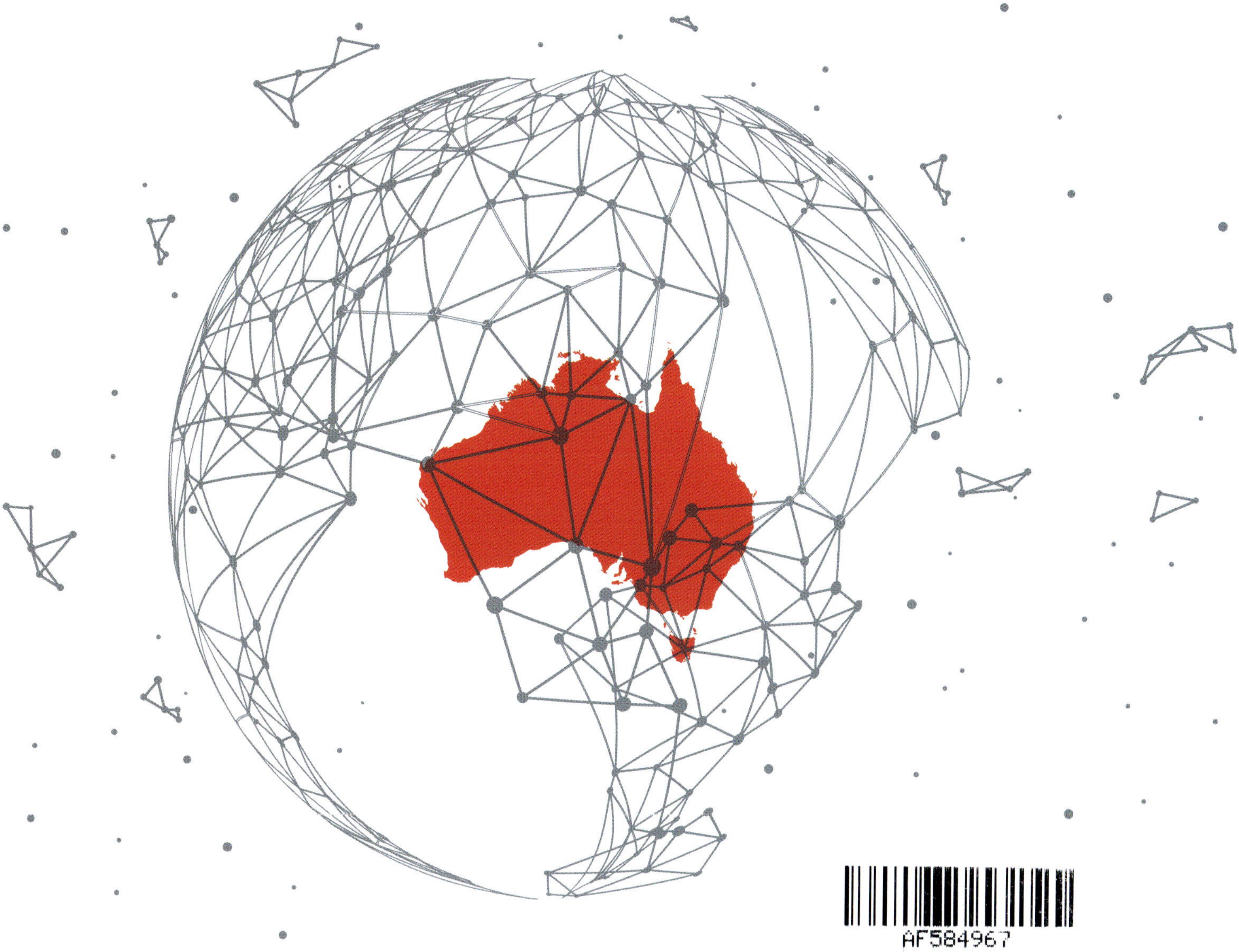

AF584967

# CLIMATE CHANGE

First Published 2025 by
Redback Publishing
Suite 6, 13a Narabang Way,
Belrose NSW 2085
Australia

www.redbackpublishing.com.au
orders@redbackpublishing.com



ISBN 978-1-761401-63-3 PBK



Author: Peter Turner
Editor: Caroline Thomas
Designer: Redback Publishing

Originated by Redback Publishing

Acknowledgements
Abbreviations: l—left, r—right, b—bottom, t—top, c—centre, m—middle
We would like to thank the following for permission to reproduce photographs: (Images © shutterstock),

p2 Iluka, NSW/ australia - November 29, 2020: kangaroos after a bushfire, by Anna LoFi, via Shutterstock.com
p9bl South Coast, NSW / Australia - January 15 2020: Baby Koala on its mother's back in the aftermath of the Australian bushfires, by Peter C 83, via Shutterstock.com, p11m Lincolnshire. United Kingdom. 07.08.13. Cooling towers of a coal-fired power plant in Lincolnshire in the United Kingdom, by Steve Allen, via Shutterstock.com, p14t Yarraville, VIC/Australia-May 8th 2018: rush hour traffic on Melbourne's West Gate Freeway, by Shuang Li, via Shutterstock.com, p27t Chernobyl, Ukraine, October 28, 2016. A group of visitors in the Control Room of the Reactor number 2 in the Chernobyl Nuclear Power Plant, by Kamil Budzynski, via Shutterstock.com, p29m Adelaide, Australia - January 13, 2017: Vegetables on display in Adelaide Central Market stall, by amophoto_au, by amophoto_au, via Shutterstock.com,

Every effort has been made to contact copyright holders of any material reproduced in this book.
Any omissions will be rectified in subsequent printings if notice is given to the publisher.

NATIONAL LIBRARY OF AUSTRALIA
A catalogue record for this book is available from the National Library of Australia

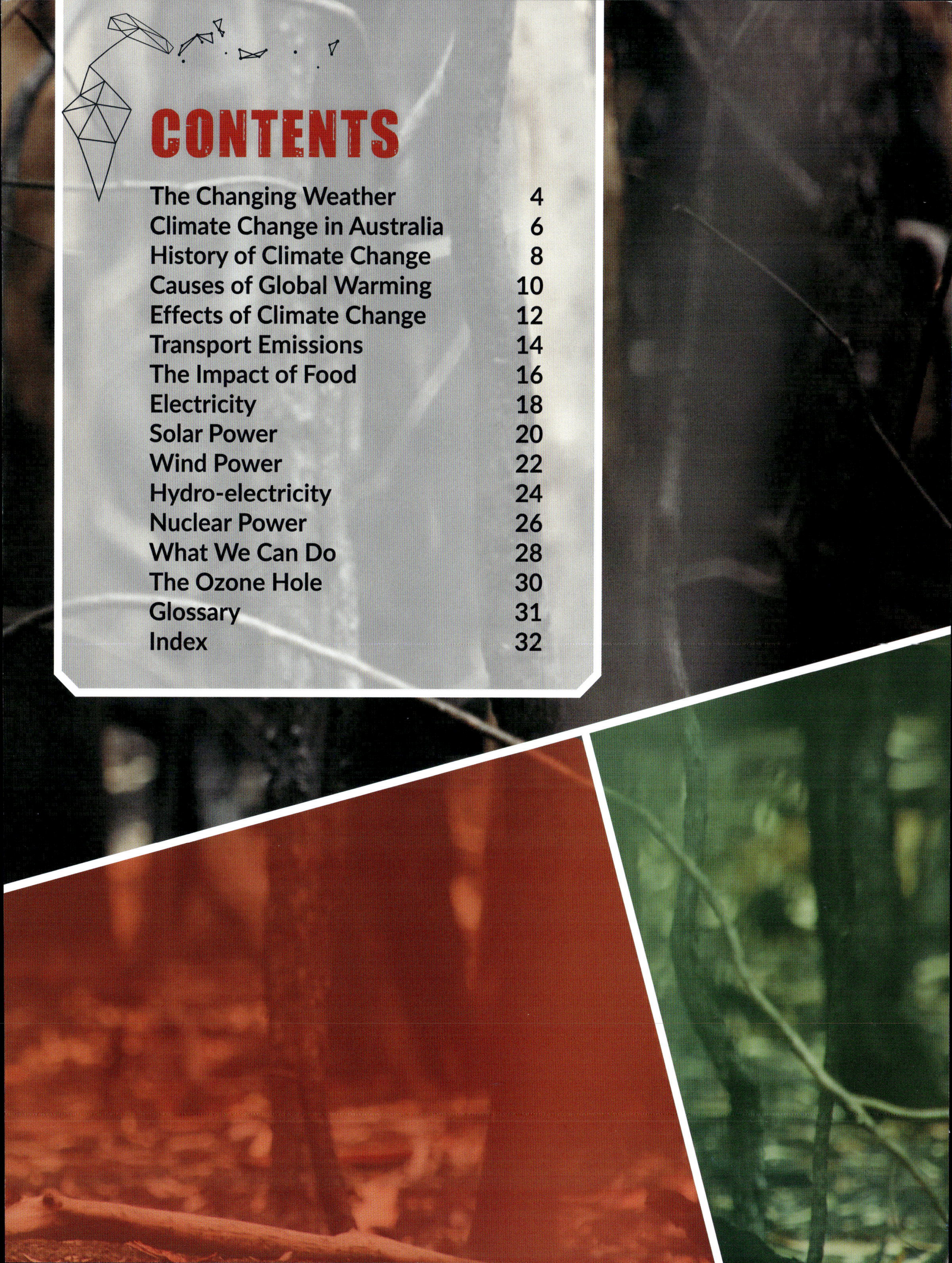

# CONTENTS

# THE CHANGING WEATHER

Weather affects every part of the planet, every day. Although the weather changes daily, it is quite consistent over longer periods. The average state of these weather conditions is known as the climate. Despite the differences in climate between countries around the world, our planet has an overall average climate.

!

Climate change can be caused by tectonic plates shifting deep beneath Earth's surface, meteors landing on Earth, or more recently by humans.

## CLIMATE CHANGE

Earth's climate has changed a number of times over 4.6 billion years. This has led to dramatic changes in the weather and to natural features such as coastlines.

# GLOBAL WARMING

Scientists have begun to notice that Earth's average temperature is rising. This phenomenon is referred to as global warming. Small temperature rises of just a few degrees can make a huge difference to Earth's climate. Rainfall patterns change, ice at the North Pole and South Pole will melt and sea levels will rise.

!

The Sun's energy supports all life on Earth. Without the Sun, Earth's temperature would drop.

## CLIMATOLOGY

Climatology is the branch of atmospheric science that is concerned with average weather patterns over longer periods of time. Climatologists look at weather patterns and extreme weather events such as hurricanes and tsunamis to predict changes in Earth's overall climate.

# CLIMATE CHANGE PREDICTIONS

## DROUGHTS

Lower rainfall in winter and spring may increase droughts

## SEA-LEVEL

Sea-levels may contine to rise

## RAINFALL

Extreme rainfall events may be likely to become more intense

## FIRE WEATHER

Harsher fire weather is expected for southern and eastern Australia

## TEMPERATURE

Temperatures may increase, with more hot days and fewer cool days

## CYCLONES

Tropical cyclones may decrease in number, but increase in intensity

## GLOBAL

Global temperatures are predicted to continue to rise

## OCEANS

Oceans around Australia may warm further and acidification may continue

# HISTORY OF CLIMATE CHANGE

## ICE AGES

Earth has experienced four major Ice Ages that covered much of the planet in thick sheets of ice. Scientists believe that the last major Ice Age ended around 10,000 years ago. Today, there is very little ice on the Earth's surface and most of it is found at the North Pole and South Pole.

!

The Earth has been changing for billions of years. There have been Ice Ages and warm periods that gave life to primitive sea anemones, dinosaurs, humans and the many animals we know today.

### 4°C

Earth's average temperature is only four degrees warmer than it was during the last Ice Age.

## CONSTANT CLIMATE

Humans, have lived on Earth for approximately 200,000 years, with many variations in climate. For the last 5,000 years, the overall climate has had an average temperature of 14 degrees Celsius. This predictability has allowed us to build homes and cities without worrying about extreme weather.

# SUDDEN WARMING

Since 1950, something strange has been happening to Earth's overall climate. In this tiny fraction of the Earth's lifetime, climatologists have found that the average temperature has increased by almost one degree. They predict that further temperature increases will happen this century. If there are increases of three or more degrees there will be serious consequences for many people.

People living along coastlines may need to move because of rising water levels, and many plant and animal species could become extinct if they cannot adapt to the changing climate.

## HABITAT LOSS

An overall climate change of just a few degrees can mean the difference between an Ice Age and a comfortable planet. Increased drought and fire are a threat to the habitats of many Australian species.

# CAUSES OF GLOBAL WARMING

Global warming is created by complex changes in the atmosphere. Human activities have caused an increase in the greenhouse gases which contribute to these changes.

## ATMOSPHERE

The atmosphere is made up of a mixture of gases, including carbon dioxide, methane, hydrogen, nitrogen and oxygen.

## WARMING

Using electricity, driving cars and producing some of the foods we eat all contribute to global warming.

## GREENHOUSE GASES

Greenhouse gases have helped to keep the Earth's temperature constant for the past 5,000 years. However, as too much greenhouse gas becomes part of the atmosphere, heat becomes trapped. This causes Earth's overall temperature to rise in a greenhouse effect.

## THE ATMOSPHERE

The ozone layer is the part of the atmosphere that absorbs most of the harmful radiation from the Sun. Earth's atmosphere acts like a tent or greenhouse, protecting the Earth from extreme levels of the Sun's radiation.

The atmosphere also traps sunlight and heat to keep Earth's surface temperature warm. It creates the environment that all life on Earth needs. Without the atmosphere, the heat from the Sun would beam directly on to the planet, making it too hot for life to exist.

## FOSSIL FUELS

Fossil fuels are stored deep in the Earth. They are made from the compressed remains of plants and animals that died millions of years ago. When these fuels burn, their stored carbon is released into the atmosphere.

# EFFECTS OF CLIMATE CHANGE

Average temperatures are increasing around the world, with recent years being some of the hottest on record. Scientists believe this is a sign that Earth's climate is changing, and they predict that further changes will happen before the end of this century.

## PREDICTIONS

Extreme weather events may increase, such as floods, tornadoes and heatwaves. More hot days and fewer cool days are expected, with less frequent rainfall that is heavier and more damaging. There may be long-term damage to our coastslines, coral reefs, rainforests, wetlands and alpine areas.

## EXTINCTION

By the end of this century, three out of five plant and animal species may be extinct due to their inability to cope with rapid environmental changes. Many countries are collecting seed samples from their plants for safe-keeping. This may provide opportunities to recreate modified versions of plants, if important varieties become extinct.

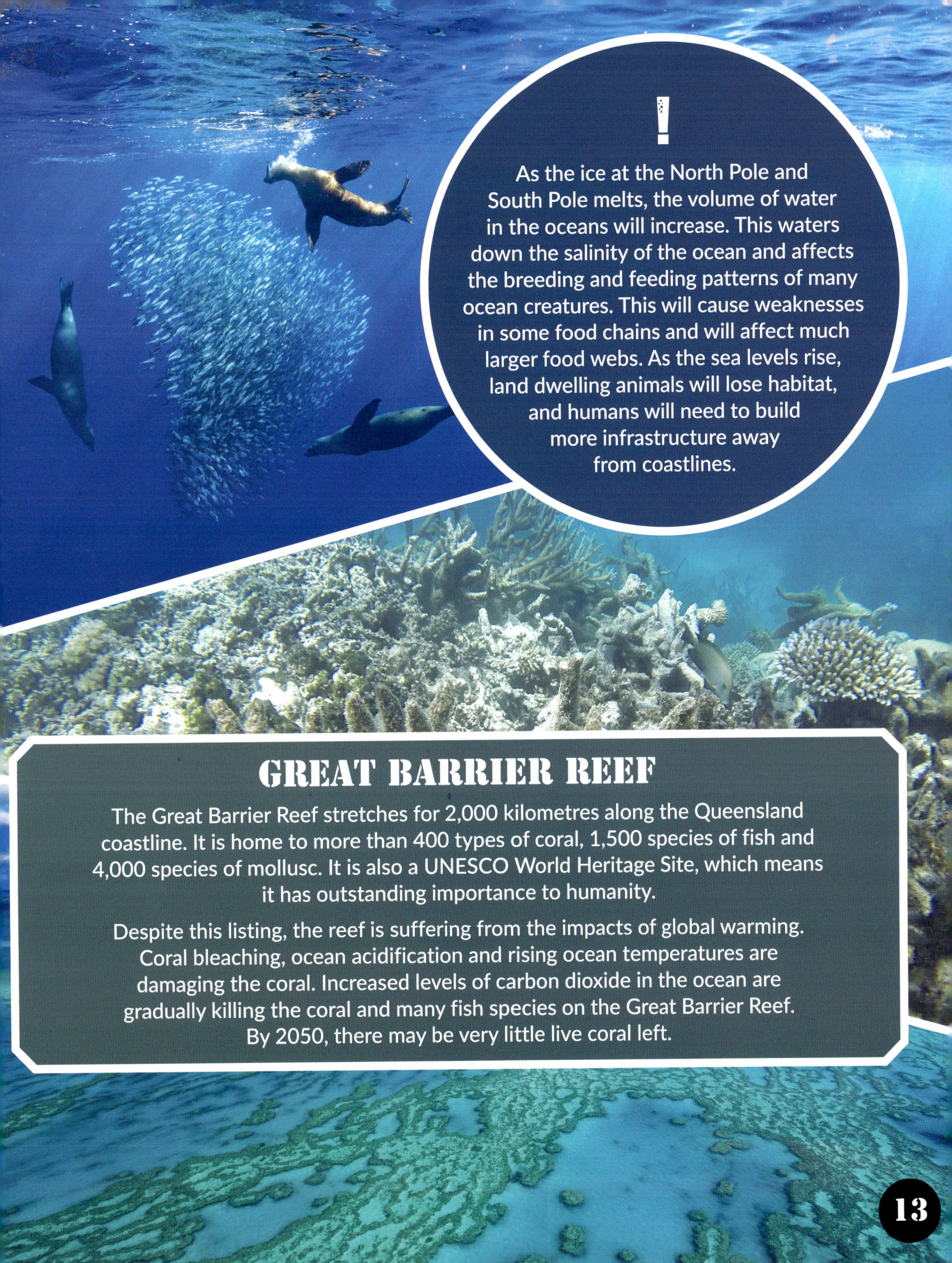

!

As the ice at the North Pole and South Pole melts, the volume of water in the oceans will increase. This waters down the salinity of the ocean and affects the breeding and feeding patterns of many ocean creatures. This will cause weaknesses in some food chains and will affect much larger food webs. As the sea levels rise, land dwelling animals will lose habitat, and humans will need to build more infrastructure away from coastlines.

## GREAT BARRIER REEF

The Great Barrier Reef stretches for 2,000 kilometres along the Queensland coastline. It is home to more than 400 types of coral, 1,500 species of fish and 4,000 species of mollusc. It is also a UNESCO World Heritage Site, which means it has outstanding importance to humanity.

Despite this listing, the reef is suffering from the impacts of global warming. Coral bleaching, ocean acidification and rising ocean temperatures are damaging the coral. Increased levels of carbon dioxide in the ocean are gradually killing the coral and many fish species on the Great Barrier Reef. By 2050, there may be very little live coral left.

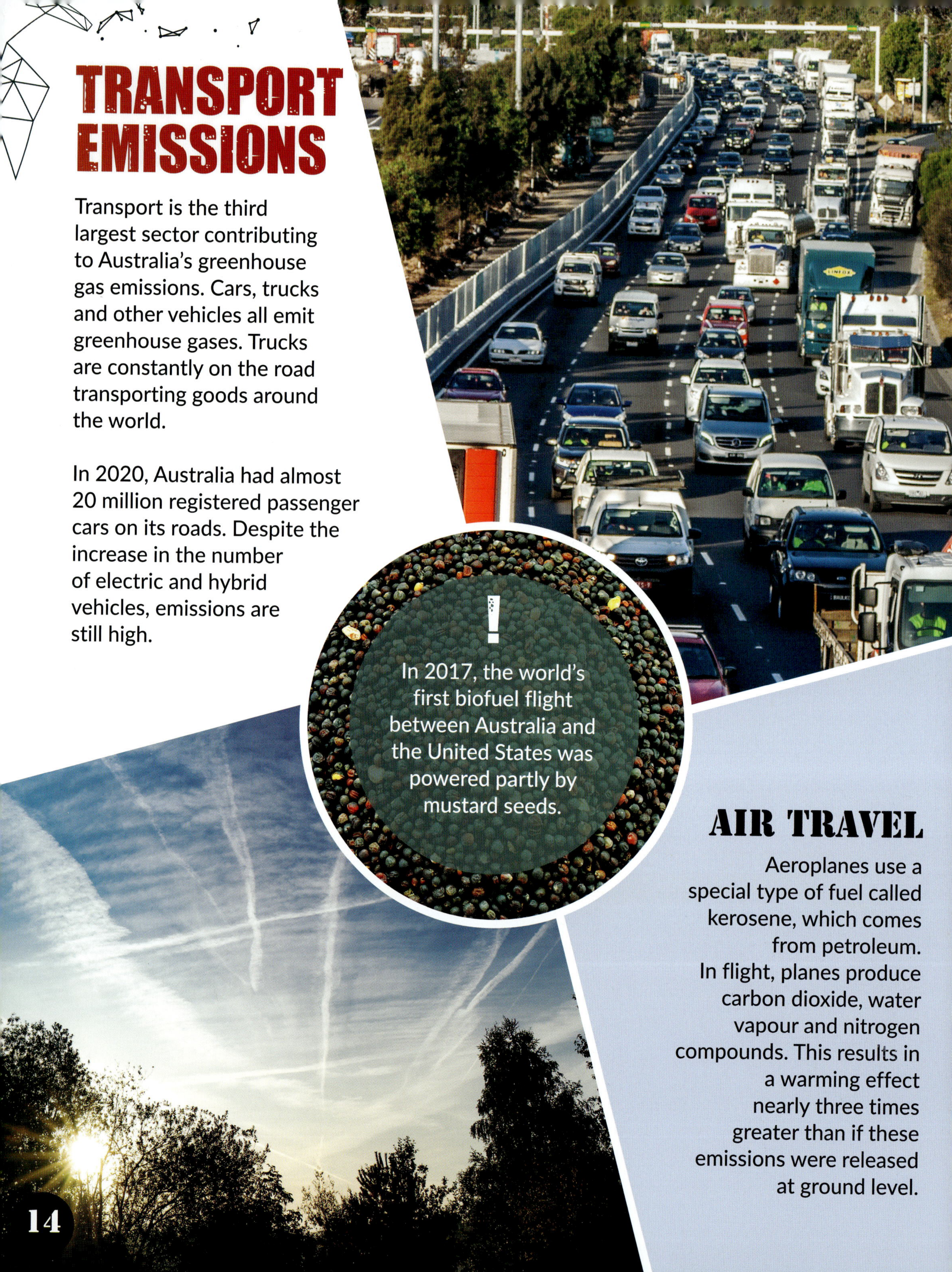

# TRANSPORT EMISSIONS

Transport is the third largest sector contributing to Australia's greenhouse gas emissions. Cars, trucks and other vehicles all emit greenhouse gases. Trucks are constantly on the road transporting goods around the world.

In 2020, Australia had almost 20 million registered passenger cars on its roads. Despite the increase in the number of electric and hybrid vehicles, emissions are still high.

!

In 2017, the world's first biofuel flight between Australia and the United States was powered partly by mustard seeds.

## AIR TRAVEL

Aeroplanes use a special type of fuel called kerosene, which comes from petroleum. In flight, planes produce carbon dioxide, water vapour and nitrogen compounds. This results in a warming effect nearly three times greater than if these emissions were released at ground level.

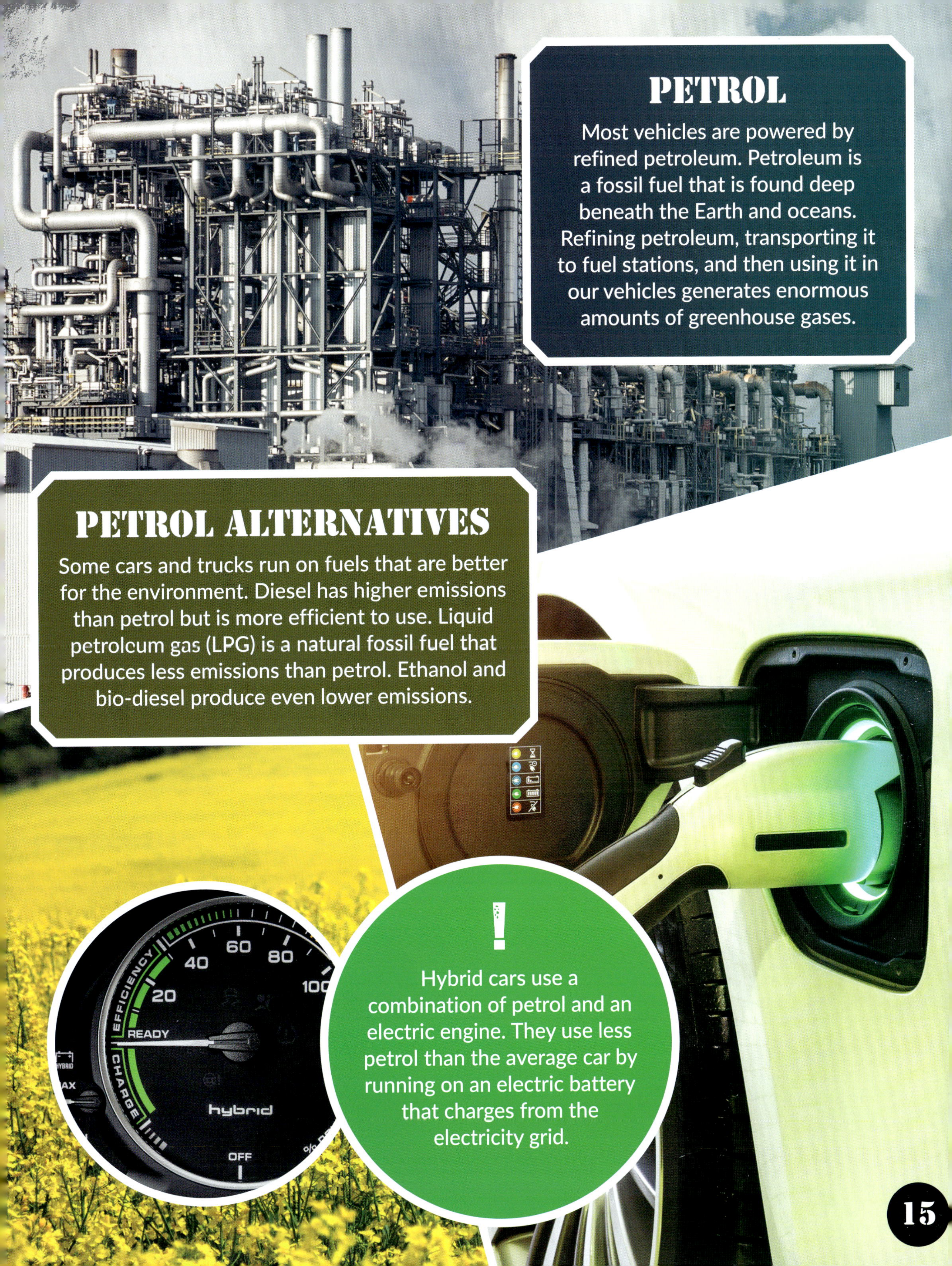


## PETROL

Most vehicles are powered by refined petroleum. Petroleum is a fossil fuel that is found deep beneath the Earth and oceans. Refining petroleum, transporting it to fuel stations, and then using it in our vehicles generates enormous amounts of greenhouse gases.

## PETROL ALTERNATIVES

Some cars and trucks run on fuels that are better for the environment. Diesel has higher emissions than petrol but is more efficient to use. Liquid petrolcum gas (LPG) is a natural fossil fuel that produces less emissions than petrol. Ethanol and bio-diesel produce even lower emissions.

!

Hybrid cars use a combination of petrol and an electric engine. They use less petrol than the average car by running on an electric battery that charges from the electricity grid.

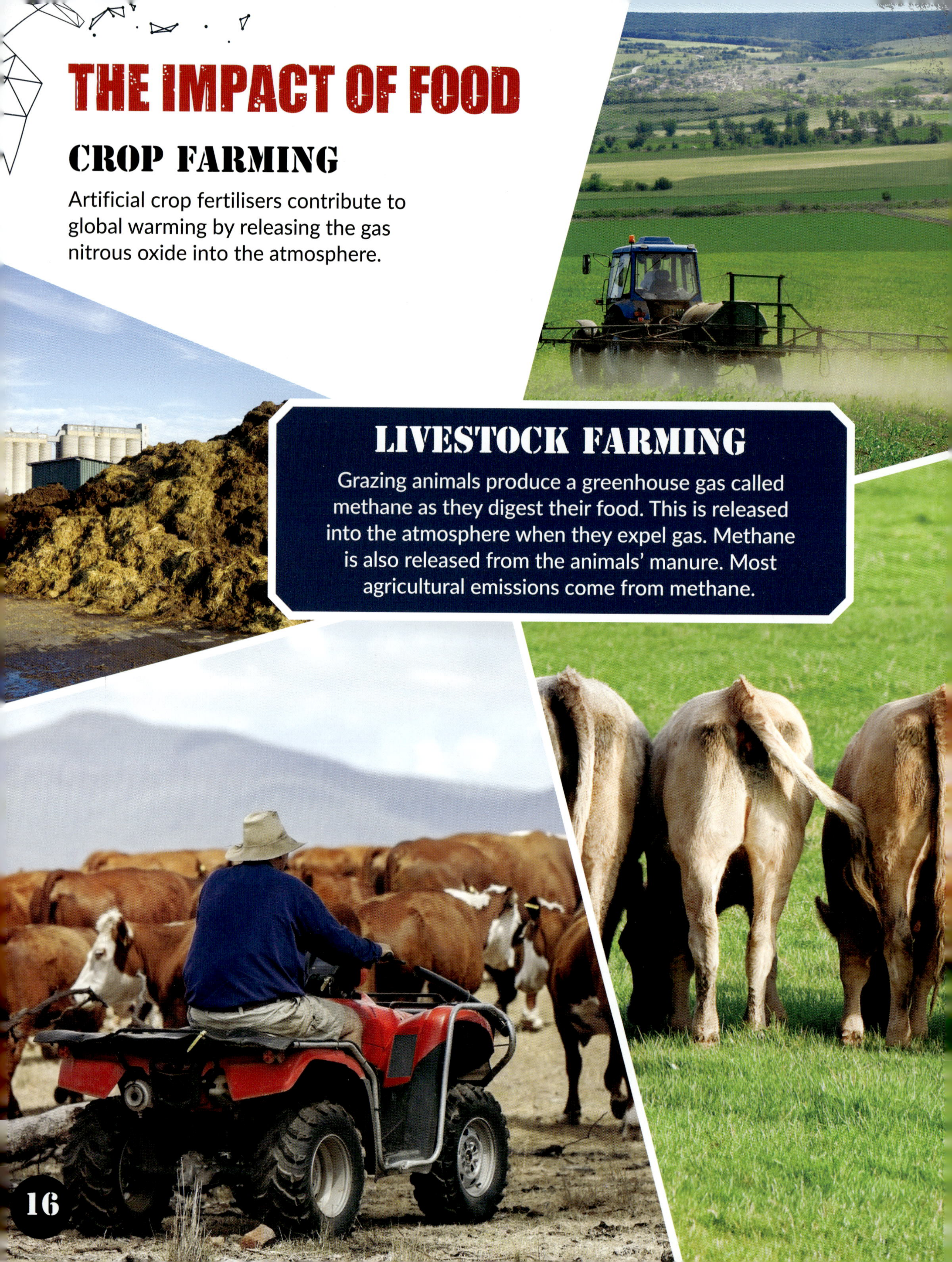

# THE IMPACT OF FOOD

## CROP FARMING

Artificial crop fertilisers contribute to global warming by releasing the gas nitrous oxide into the atmosphere.

## LIVESTOCK FARMING

Grazing animals produce a greenhouse gas called methane as they digest their food. This is released into the atmosphere when they expel gas. Methane is also released from the animals' manure. Most agricultural emissions come from methane.

# FOOD MILES

The distance that food travels before it arrives at our table is known as food miles. In the supermarket you can find tomatoes from Italy, asparagus from Peru and orange juice from Brazil. The emissions produced in getting this food to us by plane, truck or boat are significant. Eating food that has been grown or made close to where you live reduces food miles and greenhouse gas emissions.

# FOOD WASTE

When food waste breaks down in landfill sites, it releases methane into the atmosphere. In Australia, the waste that goes to landfill generates 13 million tonnes of greenhouse gas each year. Sometimes, the methane emissions from landfill waste are captured and used as fuel.

# IMPACT ON FARMING

The long-term impact of global warming may be strongly felt by the agricultural industry. It could become harder to grow crops, and extreme heat would make life tougher for the sheep, cows and pigs that live on Australian farms. Water and feed shortages may become a big problem.

# ELECTRICITY

Electricity provides us with heat and light. It powers our televisions and provides us with hot water. Although electricity can come from renewable sources, most of the world's electricity comes from burning non-renewable coal and gas, which produces large amounts of greenhouse gases.

## AC/DC

Electricity can flow as a direct current (DC), which flows in one direction, or as an alternating current (AC), which flows both backwards and forwards.

## THE GRID

Most of our electricity is produced at power stations. It is transferred to our homes through a system of wires known as the electricity grid.

## ELECTRICITY IN ACTION

Electricity results from the movement of charged particles called electrons. They create an energy current that can be channelled through a conductor, such as metal wire, so that it can be used to power electronic devices.

Electricity only flows in closed loops or circuits. When we turn off a light, we break the circuit so electricity cannot flow. When we turn the switch on again, the current flows through the circuit and the bulb lights up.

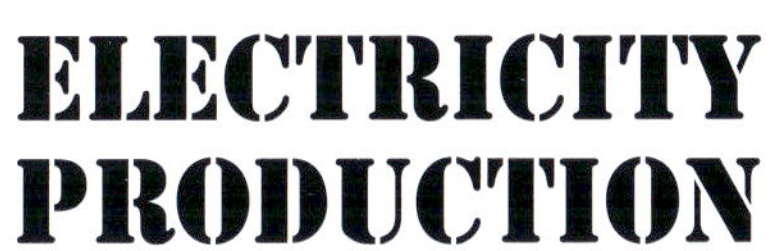

# ELECTRICITY PRODUCTION

Electricity can come from either renewable or non-renewable sources. Renewable sources include sunlight, wind and water. Most of Australia's electricity comes from non-renewable fossil fuels. Coal and gas have to be mined from the Earth before being burned in large power plants.

## STEAM POWER

Electricity can be generated by huge turbines that turn with the pressure from steam. The steam is produced by heating large amounts of water.

## NATURAL GAS

Natural gas is an odourless, colourless gas that forms beneath the ocean or land. It is mostly made up of methane, released from the remains of plants and animals that died millions of years ago. Burning natural gas produces fewer greenhouse gas emissions than burning coal.

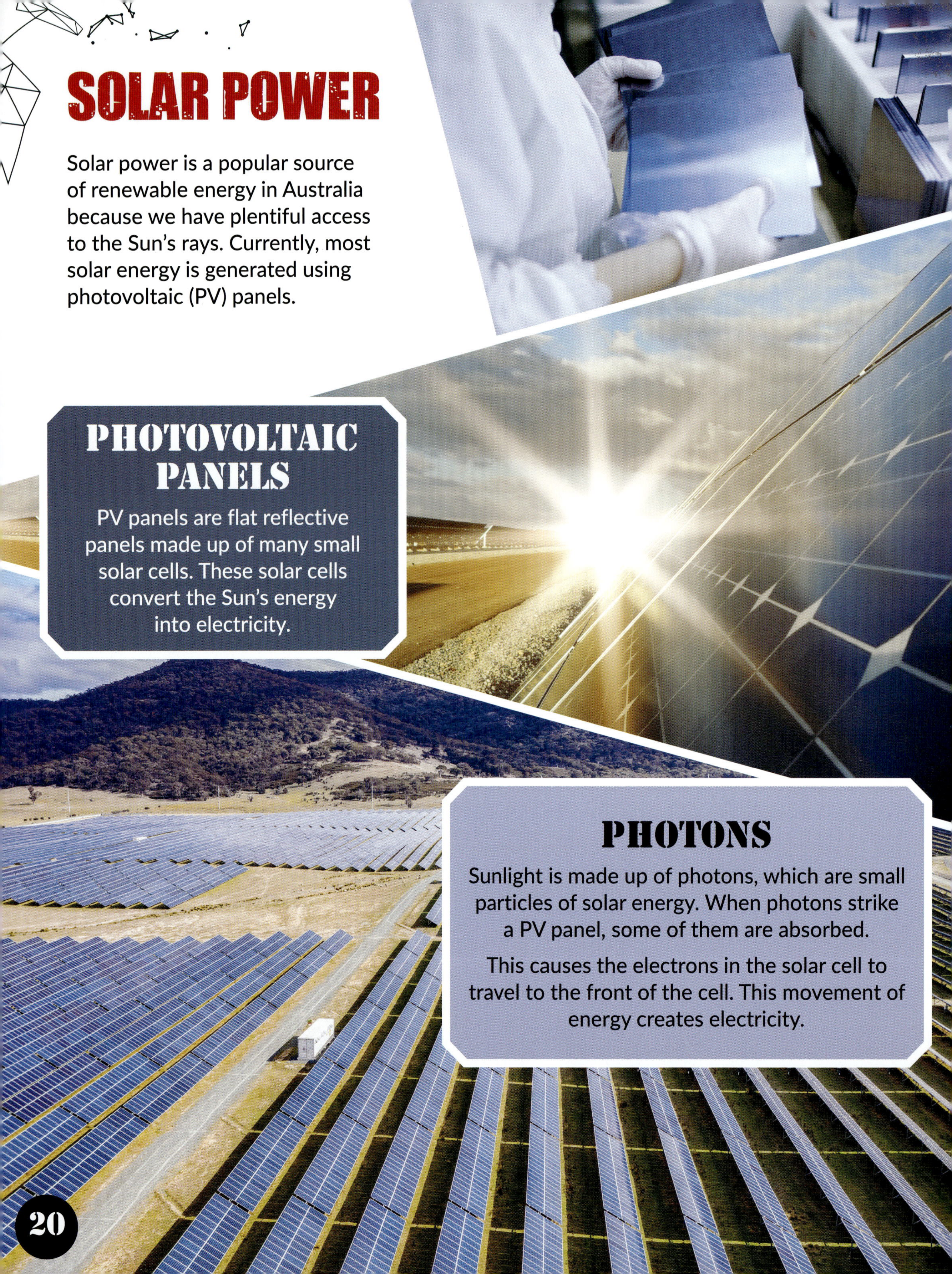

# SOLAR POWER

Solar power is a popular source of renewable energy in Australia because we have plentiful access to the Sun's rays. Currently, most solar energy is generated using photovoltaic (PV) panels.

## PHOTOVOLTAIC PANELS

PV panels are flat reflective panels made up of many small solar cells. These solar cells convert the Sun's energy into electricity.

## PHOTONS

Sunlight is made up of photons, which are small particles of solar energy. When photons strike a PV panel, some of them are absorbed.

This causes the electrons in the solar cell to travel to the front of the cell. This movement of energy creates electricity.

# SOLAR THERMAL ENERGY

Solar thermal energy harnesses the power of the Sun using lenses and mirrors. This concentrates the energy from the Sun so that it can be used to heat water to produce steam. This steam turns turbines to generate electricity.

Many of these systems use rounded panels called parabolic troughs to concentrate the Sun's energy into one area. The panels track the Sun during the day to capture as much of its energy as possible.

## POSITIVES OF SOLAR

- Solar energy produces no greenhouse gas emissions or pollution
- Energy from the Sun is free and available most days in Australia
- PV panels allow people to produce their own electricity. This is good for remote properties and reduces dependency on the electricity grid
- As fewer people depend on non-renewable energy sources, governments can shift focus to supporting infrastructure for renewable energy sources

## NEGATIVES OF SOLAR

- PV panels are currently expensive to buy and install
- PV panels need space. Privately owned panels need a large roof away from trees, or a large clear area of garden
- Making PV panels produces greenhouse emissions
- Solar energy is dependent on the Sun. It cannot be generated at night or on rainy, overcast or smoky days

# WIND POWER

Windmills have been used for thousands of years to pump water and to grind wheat into flour. This same technology is used to harness the wind to generate electricity. Wind energy is free and creates no pollution.

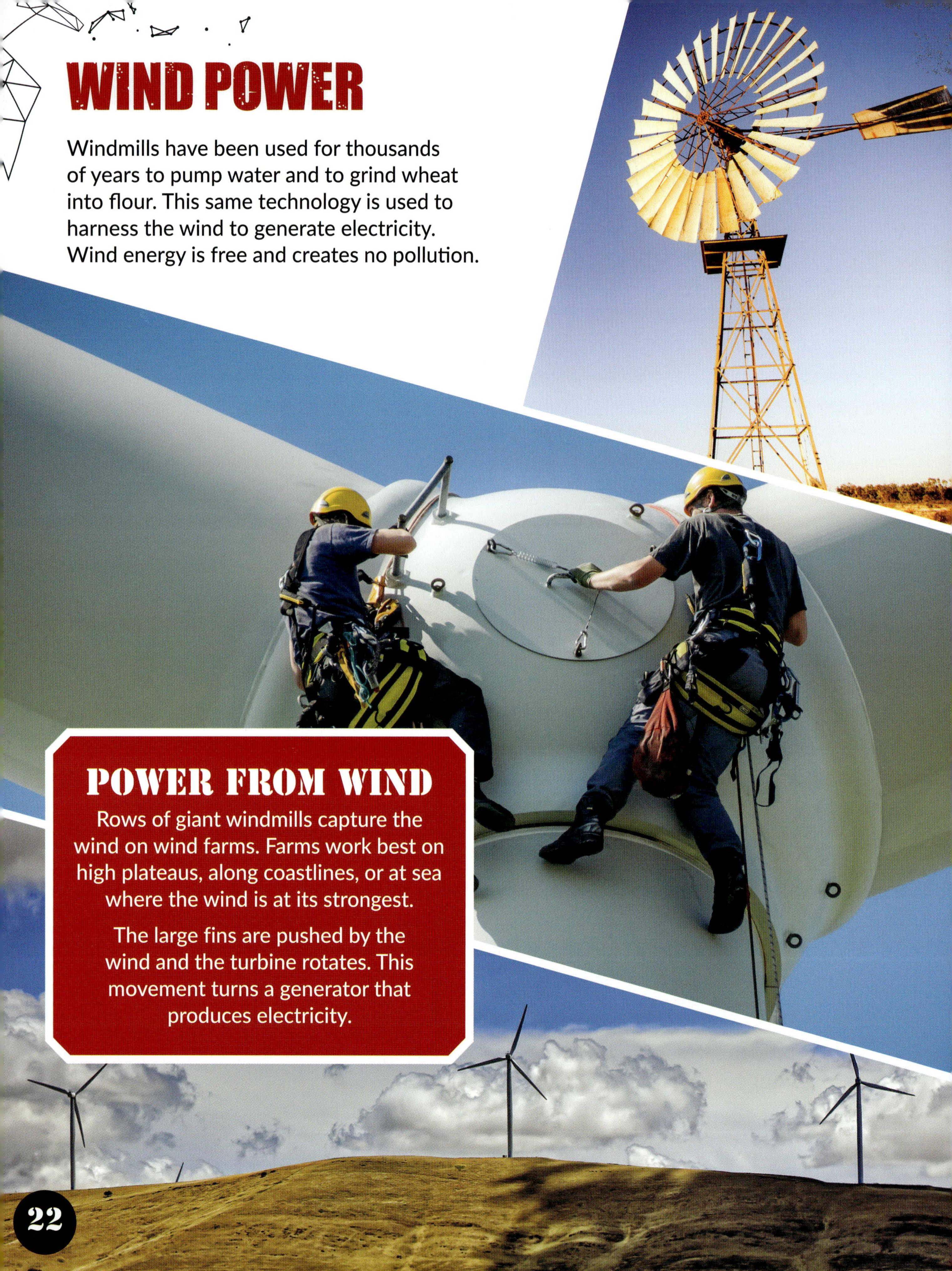

## POWER FROM WIND

Rows of giant windmills capture the wind on wind farms. Farms work best on high plateaus, along coastlines, or at sea where the wind is at its strongest.

The large fins are pushed by the wind and the turbine rotates. This movement turns a generator that produces electricity.

# WAVE ENERGY

The energy in ocean waves can be harnessed to generate electricity. The waves' power is increased by forcing the natural waves into a narrow channel to increase their size. The power of the waves turns large turbines, which generate electricity.

There are technical difficulties in capturing this energy, including the challenges of building and maintaining machinery at sea, and the naturally corrosive effect of salt water on the machinery.

## POSITIVES OF WIND POWER

- Wind turbines produce no greenhouse gases or air pollution
- Modern turbines are quiet, with their noise being about the same as background urban noise
- Wind power has few ongoing running costs
- Wind energy will never run out

## NEGATIVES OF WIND POWER

- It is not possible to generate electricity if the wind stops or slows
- Wind farms need windy areas, such as coastlines or high plateaus. These areas are usually picturesque and residents or tourism operators may not want to change the view

# HYDRO-ELECTRICITY

Hydro-electricity uses the power of moving water to generate electricity. Hydro-energy has been used for thousands of years, since rivers and streams were first used to turn a water wheel and generate power.

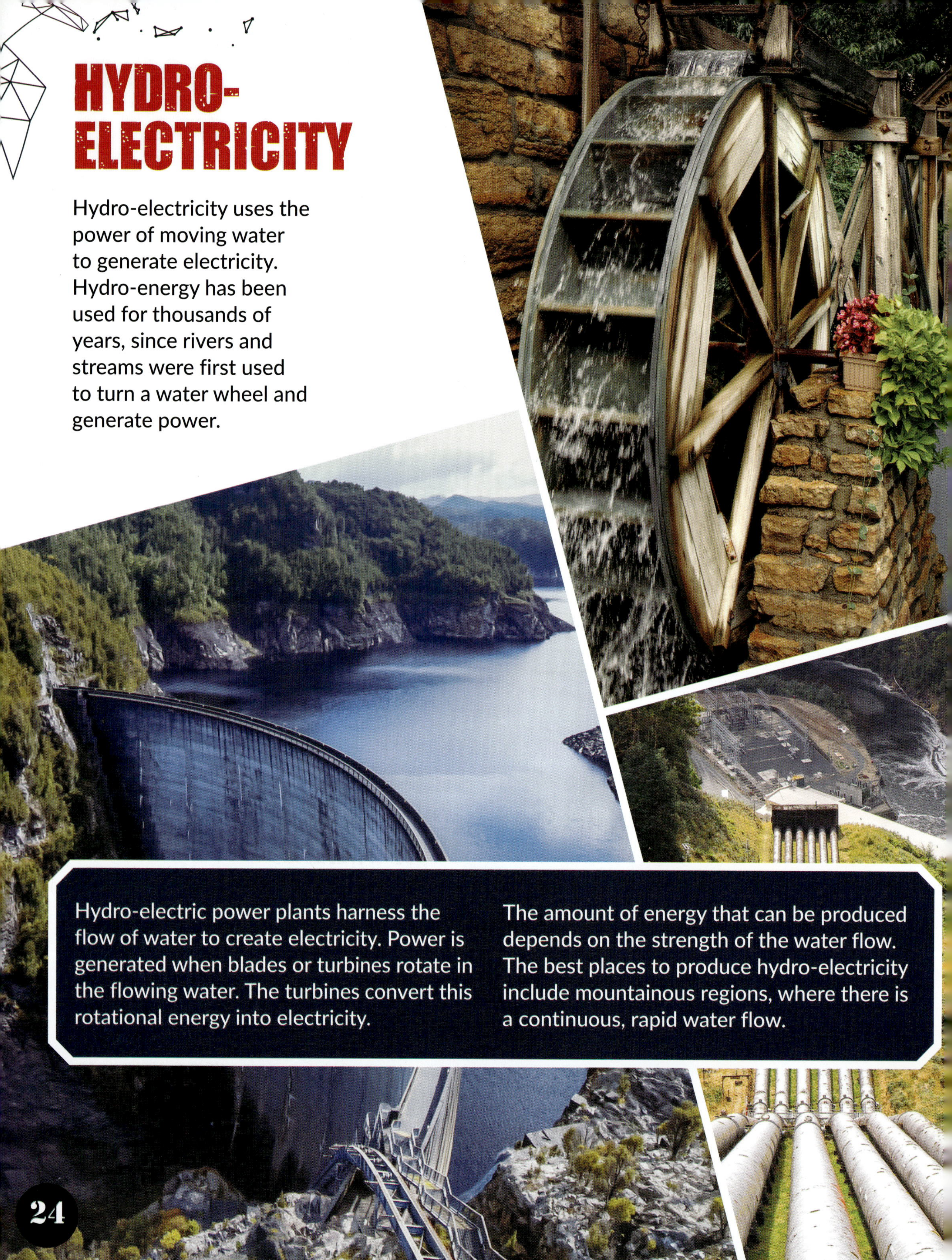

Hydro-electric power plants harness the flow of water to create electricity. Power is generated when blades or turbines rotate in the flowing water. The turbines convert this rotational energy into electricity.

The amount of energy that can be produced depends on the strength of the water flow. The best places to produce hydro-electricity include mountainous regions, where there is a continuous, rapid water flow.

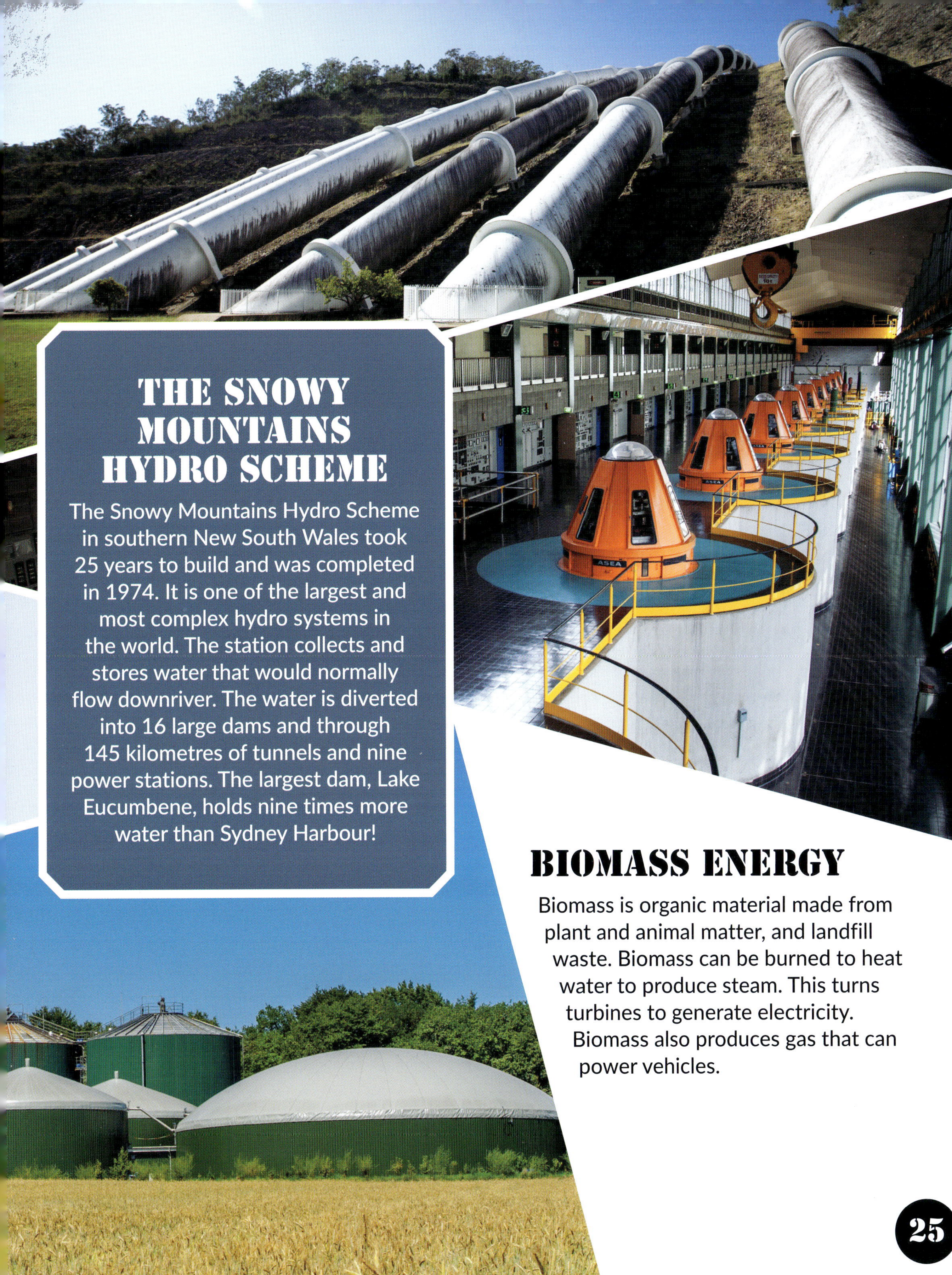


## THE SNOWY MOUNTAINS HYDRO SCHEME

The Snowy Mountains Hydro Scheme in southern New South Wales took 25 years to build and was completed in 1974. It is one of the largest and most complex hydro systems in the world. The station collects and stores water that would normally flow downriver. The water is diverted into 16 large dams and through 145 kilometres of tunnels and nine power stations. The largest dam, Lake Eucumbene, holds nine times more water than Sydney Harbour!

## BIOMASS ENERGY

Biomass is organic material made from plant and animal matter, and landfill waste. Biomass can be burned to heat water to produce steam. This turns turbines to generate electricity. Biomass also produces gas that can power vehicles.

# NUCLEAR POWER

The nuclear power cycle begins with the mining of uranium. This uranium is then processed into enriched uranium-235. Uranium-235 atoms can be split in a nuclear reactor to release massive amounts of energy. This process is called nuclear fission.

Nuclear fission provides up to three million times more energy than coal. This energy is harnessed as steam, which is used to drive a turbine and produce electricity.

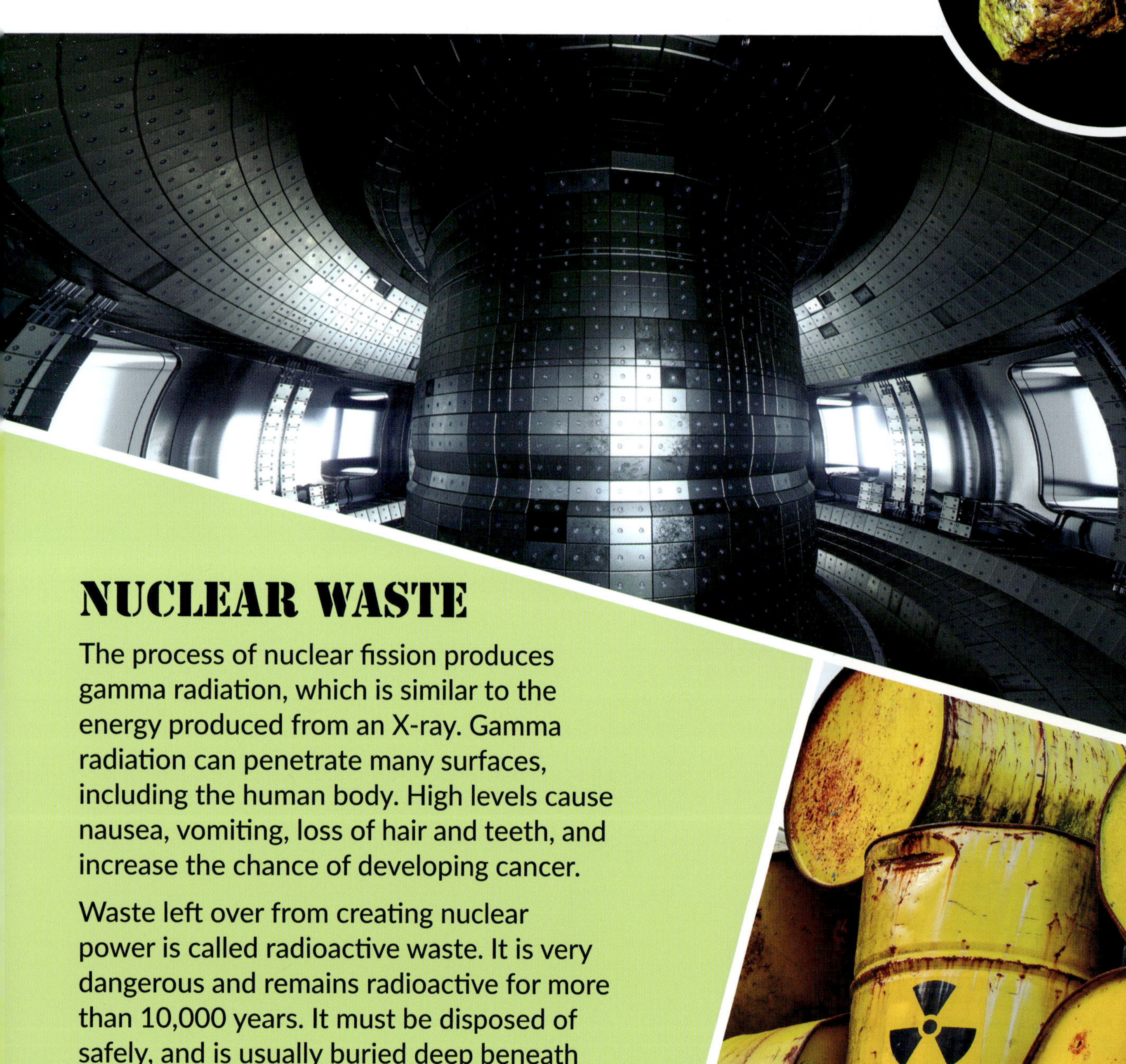

## NUCLEAR WASTE

The process of nuclear fission produces gamma radiation, which is similar to the energy produced from an X-ray. Gamma radiation can penetrate many surfaces, including the human body. High levels cause nausea, vomiting, loss of hair and teeth, and increase the chance of developing cancer.

Waste left over from creating nuclear power is called radioactive waste. It is very dangerous and remains radioactive for more than 10,000 years. It must be disposed of safely, and is usually buried deep beneath the ground or sea.

## CHERNOBYL

In 1986, there was a massive explosion at the Chernobyl Nuclear Power Plant in northern Ukraine. Operators had disconnected safety circuits to perform tests on the reactor. This made it unstable and when they tried to put the circuits back, a huge amount of nuclear energy was released. A series of explosions threw radioactive material out of the building and into the surrounding areas.

Wind and rain spread radioactive particles throughout Europe, reaching over 3,000 kilometres away. The official death toll was 3,600 people, but the United Nations estimates that over 5 million people in Europe were exposed to radioactive particles. Today, over 2,500 square kilometres of land are still dangerously contaminated. This land is in an exclusion zone which will not be safe to enter for at least another 250 years.

## FUKUSHIMA

In March 2011, Japan suffered a massive earthquake that triggered a devastating tsunami. It disabled the power supply and cooling of three Fukushima Daiichi reactors and caused a serious nuclear accident. High levels of radiation were released into Japan's environment, food supply and surrounding ocean.

## POSITIVES OF NUCLEAR POWER

- Australia has large amounts of uranium
- Nuclear power can produce huge amounts of electricity
- Nuclear power plants create no greenhouse gas emissions
- Once a nuclear power plant is set up, the running costs are low

## NEGATIVES OF NUCLEAR POWER

- In Australia, nuclear power plants would need to be built close to seawater, for use in cooling. Suitable sites all include heavily populated areas or tourist destinations
- Most of Australia's uranium is found in environmentally significant areas, such as Kakadu National Park, where mining would not be welcomed

# WHAT WE CAN DO

According to the World Bank, Australia's carbon footprint is three times the global average.

Standby / On

## DO NOT STANDBY

Turn appliances off at the wall when you are finished with them to reduce the carbon footprint of your home. Some appliances in standby mode use nearly the same amount of electricity as when they are turned on.

## UPGRADE

We can significantly reduce our carbon footprint by upgrading appliances to newer, more energy efficient models. We can turn off lights when not in use and switch to energy efficient light globes. We can choose electricity from renewable sources by buying it from an accredited 'green power' supplier. This increases investment in renewable energy sources and reduces our reliance on coal.

## WALK OR USE PUBLIC TRANSPORT

Motor vehicle emissions are sources of airborne pollution. Walking or riding a bicycle are cleaner transport choices. Public transport produces less pollution than personal transport such as cars.

## COMPOSTING

Food scraps account for more than 40 percent of household rubbish. They end up as landfill, giving off methane and carbon dioxide as they break down. Compost bins, worm farms and keeping chickens can significantly reduce the amount of waste going to landfill.

## BUY LOCAL

Transporting foods produces huge amounts of emissions. Choosing locally grown produce supports local farmers and reduces transport emissions.

## FOOD

Livestock such as cows and sheep release huge amounts of methane into the environment. In addition, trees are cleared to provide pasture for these grazing animals. When we eat meat and dairy, we are increasing the demand for more livestock animals.

# THE OZONE HOLE

Ozone is an atmospheric gas that protects Earth from dangerous radiation from the Sun. Chlorofluorocarbons, or CFCs, are used in aerosol cans, fridges, foam and some air conditioners. CFCs destroy ozone in the atmosphere, and they are also greenhouse gases.

In 1984, scientists discovered a hole in the ozone layer of the atmosphere over Antarctica, and they began work to stop this ozone hole getting any larger. This action led to the creation of The Montreal Protocol, which governments around the world signed in 1987. Since then, the total use of CFCs has decreased by 90 percent. The 'hole' in the ozone is now shrinking, but parts of southern Australia, New Zealand and Antarctica still have high levels of dangerous UV radiation because of the lack of ozone in the atmosphere.

## INTERNATIONAL LAWS

Over the past 30 years, major international treaties have been signed to combat the effects of ozone depletion and global warming.

One of the most successful international agreements is the Montreal Protocol on Substances that Deplete the Ozone Layer.

# GLOSSARY

**atmosphere** gases that surround Earth

**biomass** organic matter used to generate electricity

**carbon dioxide** greenhouse gas produced by burning fossil fuels

**carbon footprint** total greenhouse gas emissions caused by an individual or business

**chlorofluorocarbon** (CFC) greenhouse gas used in some aerosol cans and air conditioners

**climate change** overall changes to a climate due to changes in average temperature

**contaminate** make something impure by mixing harmful substances into it

**drought** period of little or no rainfall

**emissions** release of greenhouse gases into the atmosphere

**fossil fuels** coal, oil and gas are from the ancient remains of plants and animals

**global warming** increase in the overall temperature of the planet

**greenhouse gases** gases that trap the Sun's heat – carbon dioxide, methane, nitrous oxide

**methane** greenhouse gas released by grazing cattle and at landfill sites

**petroleum** fossil fuel found deep beneath the Earth and oceans

**photovoltaic panels** reflective solar cells that convert the Sun's energy to electricity

**radioactive** emitting unsafe subatomic particles that can harm living things

# INDEX